THE ARCTIC OCEAN (p. 3)

THE ARCTIC OCEAN (p. 2)

ON THE PACK ICE (p. 4)

CLIFF DWELLING BIRDS (p. 5)

POLAR ANIMALS
A STICKER FUN® BOOK

Lands of ice and snow, bare mountains and flat plains called tundra; these are the lands of the polar regions. You'll be surprised to see how many hardy plants and animals can survive this cruel climate. Remove the sticker pages from the book and press out the stickers carefully. Moisten and stick in place on the pages where they belong. You may want to color the rest of each page lightly with colored pencil or crayon. It's fun to learn the names of the many arctic animals and plants. Keep this book as your guide.

Copyright © 1983 Western Publishing Company, Inc.
All rights reserved.

GOLDEN®, GOLDEN® & DESIGN, A GOLDEN BOOK®, and STICKER FUN®
are trademarks of Western Publishing Company, Inc.

A GOLDEN® BOOK
Western Publishing Company, Inc.
Racine, Wisconsin 53404
No part of this book may be reproduced or copied in any form without written permission from the publisher. Produced in U.S.A.

THE ARCTIC OCEAN

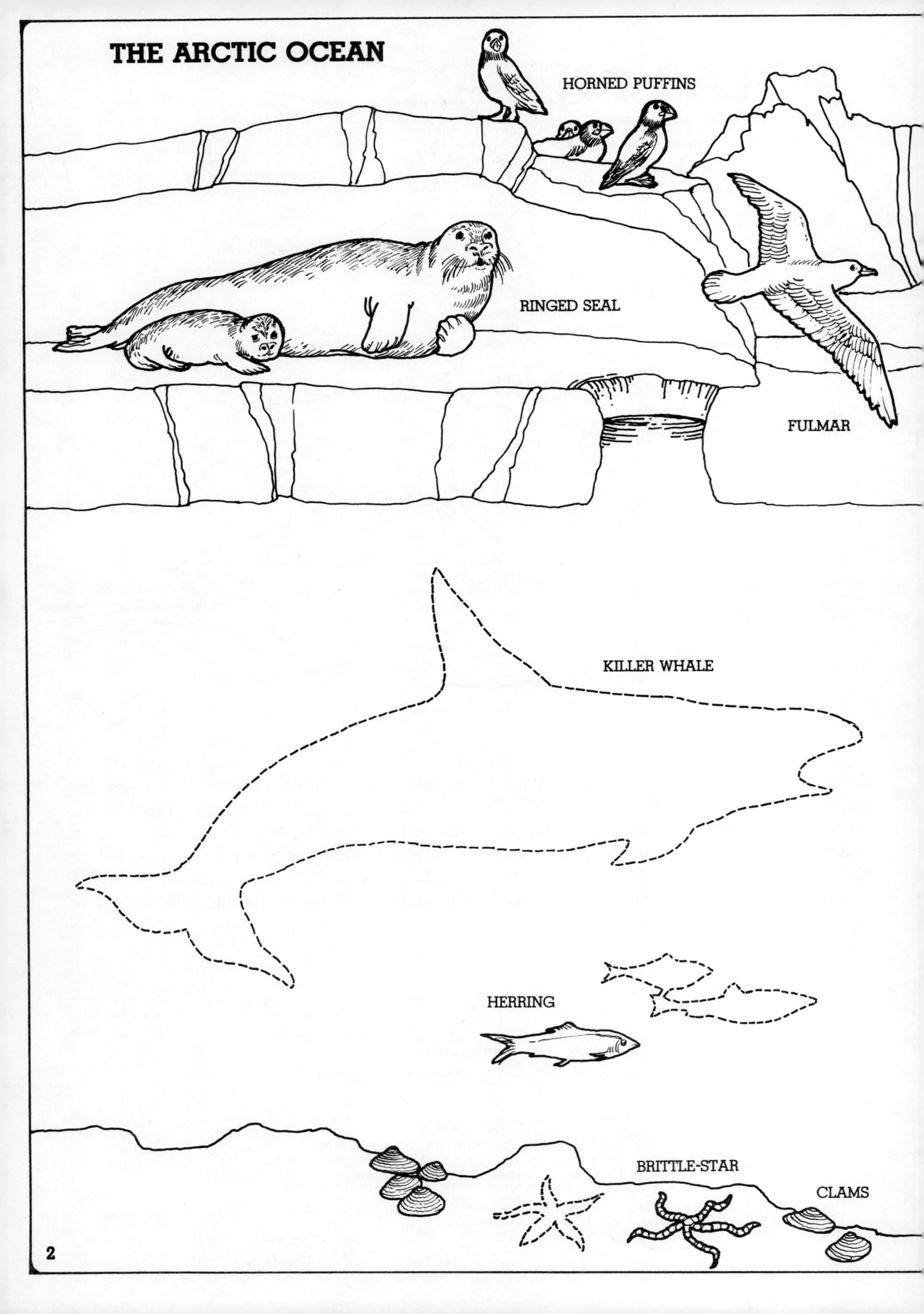

HORNED PUFFINS

RINGED SEAL

FULMAR

KILLER WHALE

HERRING

BRITTLE-STAR

CLAMS

SABINE GULL

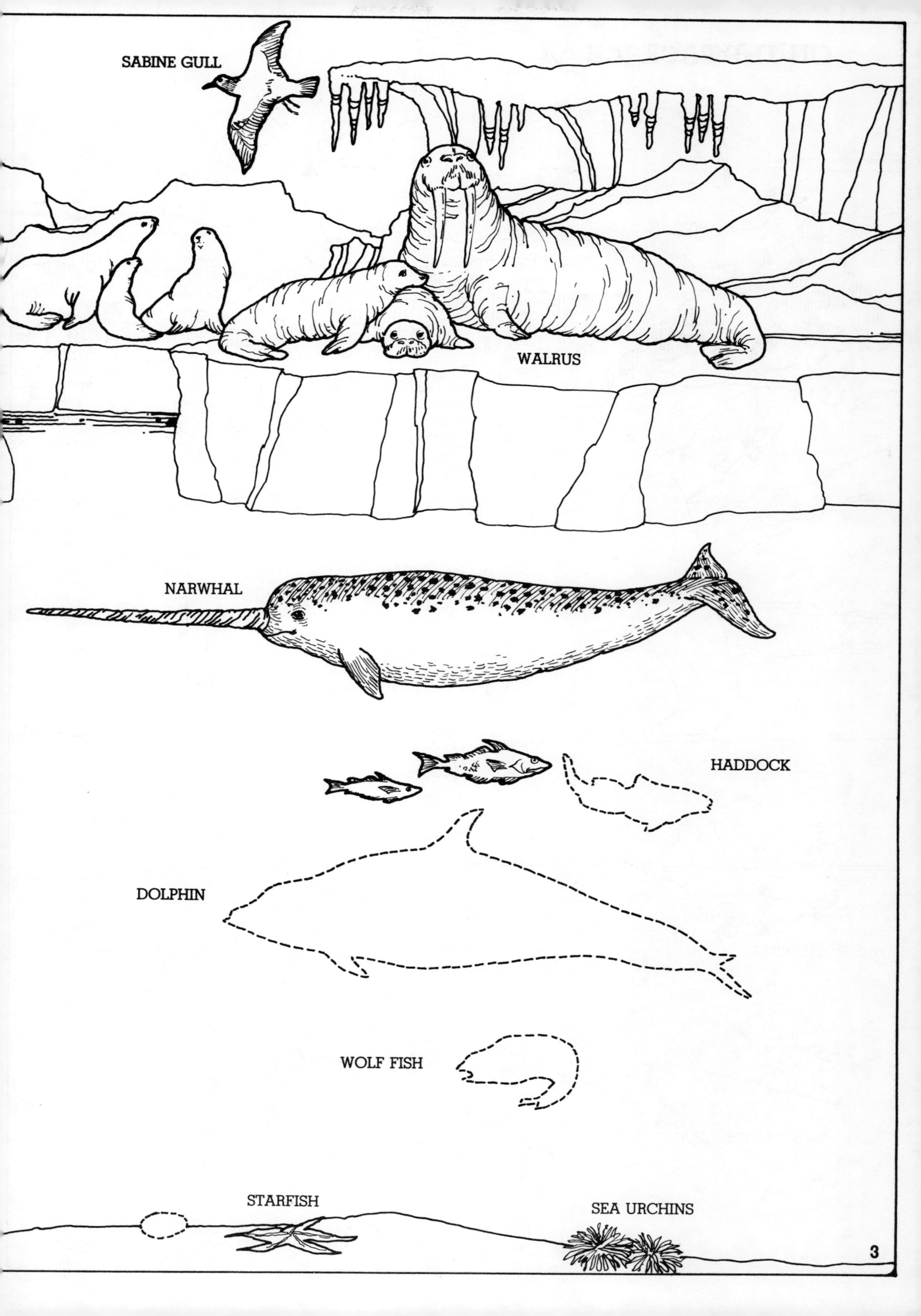

WALRUS

NARWHAL

HADDOCK

DOLPHIN

WOLF FISH

STARFISH

SEA URCHINS

3

ON THE PACK ICE

POLAR BEAR

HERRING

BEARDED SEAL

HADDOCK

4

CLIFF DWELLING BIRDS

BLACK CORMORANTS

NORTHERN GANNETS

PUFFINS

FULMARS

5

A CLOSER LOOK AT THE TUNDRA

RED FOX

HOARY MARMOT

PIKA

WILLOW PTARMIGAN

MOSS CHAMPION

ARCTIC SQUIRREL

TUNDRA STREAM

MOOSE

BEAR CUBS

MINK

BROWN BEAR

COTTON GRASS

MARSH VIOLETS

TUNDRA GRASSLANDS (p. 10)

TUNDRA GRASSLANDS (p. 11)

TUNDRA STREAM (p. 8)

THE MOUNTAIN TUNDRA (p. 9)

A CLOSER LOOK AT THE TUNDRA (p. 6)

A CLOSER LOOK AT THE TUNDRA (p. 7)

FOREST TUNDRA (p. 12)

FOREST TUNDRA (p. 13)

THE MOUNTAIN TUNDRA

DALL SHEEP

ARCTIC HARE

TUNDRA GRASSLANDS

MOOSE

CARIBOU

SANDHILL CRANE

LOON

10

ARCTIC WOLVES

MUSK OX

ARCTIC SQUIRREL

ARCTIC WILLOW

ARCTIC POPPY

11

FOREST TUNDRA

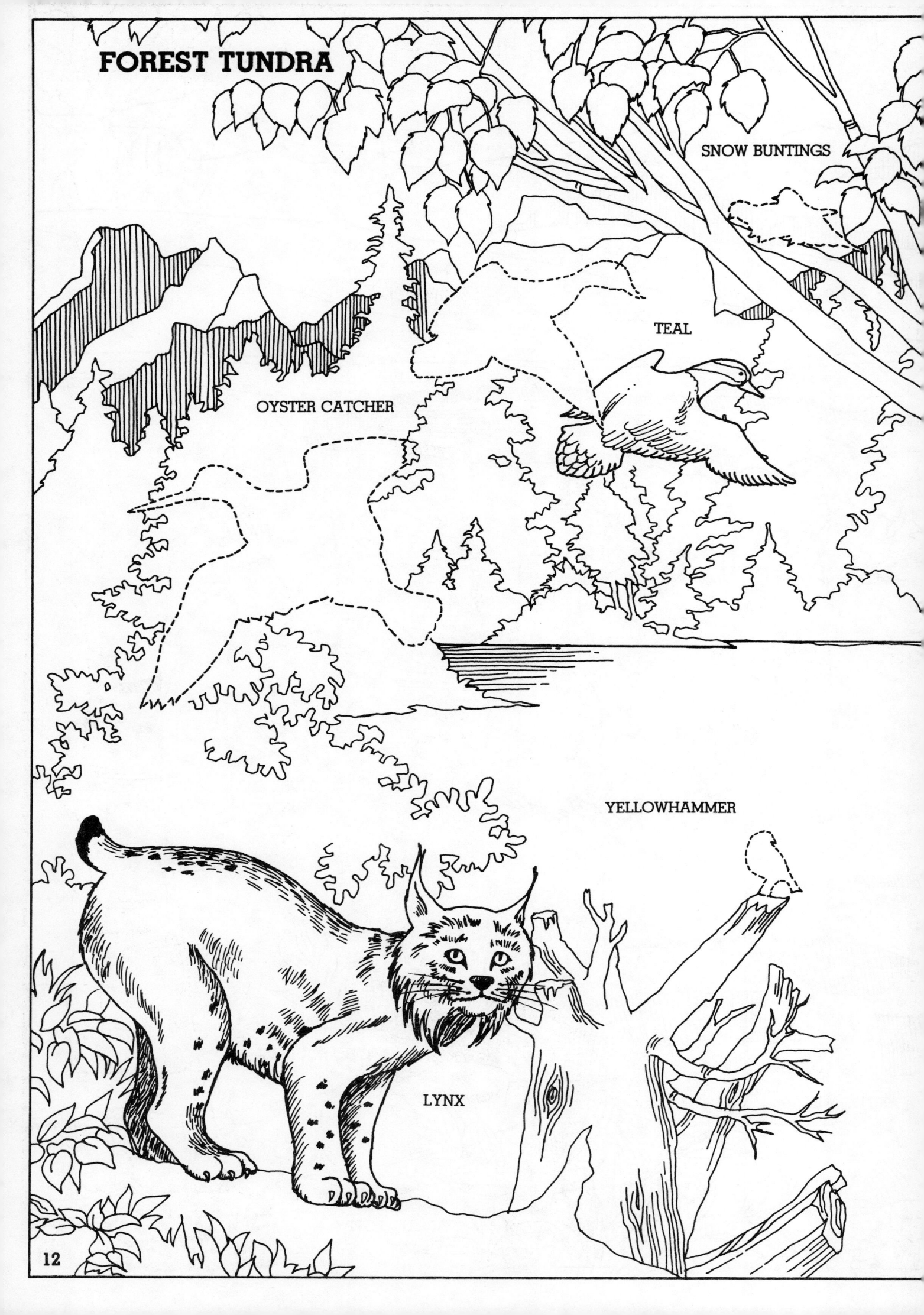

SNOW BUNTINGS

TEAL

OYSTER CATCHER

YELLOWHAMMER

LYNX

12

GREAT GREY OWL

RED-BREASTED GOOSE

RED POLE

OTTER

DARK-FURRED MARTEN

13

THE ARCTIC FOX

ARCTIC FOX

CROWBERRY CINQUEFOIL SAXIFRAGE

LEMMINGS

THE SNOWY OWL

LONG-TAILED JAEGER

SNOWY OWL

LEMMING

LUPINE

15

SEA DUCKS

GOOSEANDER DUCK

GOLDEN EYE DUCK

HARLEQUIN DUCKS

STELLER'S EIDER DUCKS

RED-BREASTED MERGANSERS

16

THE SNOWY OWL (p. 15)

THE ARCTIC FOX (p. 14)

SEA DUCKS (p. 16)